Rookie Read-About® Science

It Could Still Be A Dog

By Allan Fowler

Consultants:
Robert L. Hillerich, Professor Emeritus,
Bowling Green State University, Bowling Green, Ohio
Consultant, Pinellas County Schools, Florida

Lynn Kepler, Educational Consultant

Fay Robinson, Child Development Specialist

CHILDRENS PRESS®
CHICAGO

Design by Beth Herman Design Associates

Library of Congress Cataloging-in-Publication Data

Fowler, Allan.
    It could still be a dog / by Allan Fowler.
      p. cm. –(Rookie read-about science)
    Summary: Describes the various sizes and shapes of different types of dogs
and some of the jobs they do.
    ISBN 0-516-06016-3
    1. Dogs–Juvenile literature. [1. Dogs.] I. Title. II. Series: Fowler, Allan.
Rookie read-about science.
SF426.5.F69   1993
636.7–dc20   93-880
                                                 CIP
                                                   AC

Do you have a dog?
You're very lucky if
you do.

A dog will be your friend
if you love it,

and take good care of it,

and play with it – when
the dog wants to play.

Some dogs like to chase balls. Some dogs catch Frisbees.

Puppies like playing with other puppies.

Dogs come in many different sizes, shapes, and colors.

A dog could be as big
as a Great Dane

or as small as a Chihuahua,
and still be a dog.

A dog could have long
legs and a lean body, like
a speedy greyhound,

or short legs and a long
body, like a dachshund or
a basset hound, and it
could still be a dog.

A dog might be as cute as a
Yorkshire terrier, a Scottie,

or a Lhasa apso.

It might look as fierce as an English bulldog. But bulldogs are really very gentle. They only look fierce.

A dog could be covered
with spots, like a dalmatian,

have a long, silky coat,
like a cocker spaniel,

or be clipped to look fancy,
like this poodle, and still
be a dog.

Some dogs work for their owners. Dogs that are trained to guide blind people are called seeing eye dogs.

A dog could help the police,
like this German shepherd,

pull a sled, like a husky,

or take care of sheep, like a sheepdog or collie, and still be a dog.

Beagles and bloodhounds
have a great sense of smell.
They use their nose to
follow an animal's trail.

Each of these kinds of dogs is called a breed. There are many breeds.

A purebred dog is one that belongs to a single breed.

But lots of dogs are mixed
breeds. Their parents were
different kinds of dogs.

A mixed breed dog can be just as smart, lovable, and loyal as a purebred dog.

So whether your dog is a
purebred or a mixed breed...

trained to do work or kept
as a pet...

a brand-new puppy or
fully grown...

it could still be one of your
best friends.

Words You Know

English bulldog   cocker spaniel   poodle

German shepherd   greyhound

Great Dane   mixed breed   huskies

basset hounds

beagle

collie

dachshund

dalmatian

Yorkshire terrier

Chihuahua

Scottie

Lhasa apso

Index

About the Author

Allan Fowler is a free-lance writer with a background in advertising. Born in New York, he lives in Chicago now and enjoys traveling.

Photo Credits

Animals Animals – ©Susan L. Jones, 10, 30 (bottom left)

©Noriva Behling – 26

©Kent & Donna Dannen – 20

PhotoEdit – ©Myrleen Ferguson, 3

©Reynolds Photography – 12, 30 (center right)

SuperStock International, Inc. – ©W. Hamilton, 5; ©Zaremba, 6; ©Beerman Collection, 7; ©The Photo Source, 16, 30 (top left); ©P. Ramaekers, 19, 24, 30 (top right), 31 (top center)

Valan – ©Eastcott/Momatiuk, 4, 22, 29, 30 (bottom right); ©J.A. Wilkinson, Cover, 8, 31 (top left); Kennon Cooke, 11, 14, 23, 31 (bottom left), 31 (center right); ©Herman H. Giethoorn, 13, 15, 18, 27, 30 (top center, bottom center), 31 (center left, bottom center, bottom right); ©Allan Wilkinson, 17, 31(top right), 31 (center center); ©J.R. Page, 21, 30 (center left)

COVER: Bassett hounds